INTRODUCTION

The Hill House was built in 1902–3 by Charles Rennie Mackintosh, arguably Scotland's most famous architect and designer. Commissioned by the Glasgow publisher Walter Blackie, it remains a remarkably complete example of Mackintosh's unique vision. It is also widely acclaimed as a work of art and design associated with the Art Nouveau movement at the turn of the 20th century.

Attracting hundreds of thousands of visitors from all over the globe, the Hill House has gained an iconic status as one of the world's most celebrated houses. Since 1982 it has been in the care of the National Trust for Scotland, whose aim has been to return the house to its original state. However, balancing curatorial and conservation needs with the welcoming of 30,000 visitors a year presents a challenge and requires careful day-to-day management of the building. A programme of research in collaboration with Historic Scotland has yielded many exciting and controversial discoveries, as well as making a significant contribution to our knowledge and understanding of Mackintosh interiors.

The numbers who make the pilgrimage to the Hill House every year testify to the tremendous popularity Mackintosh's work now enjoys. But it was not always so – in his lifetime his work received little appreciation, at least in Britain. The rehabilitation of his reputation reached its peak in the 1990s, and today visitors to this house engage with his work on an emotional, intellectual, sensual and imaginative level. The diversity of the appeal of the Hill House speaks volumes about the depth of Mackintosh's creative gift, and in this guidebook we explore how he 'made it all work'.

CREATING A VISION

The west facade of the house under construction, 6 June 1903

Opposite: the house shortly after its completion in 1904

'Here is the house. It is not an Italian Villa, an English Mansion House, a Swiss Chalet, or a Scotch Castle. It is a Dwelling House.'
(Walter Blackie, *Memories*, 1943)

With these engagingly blunt words, Charles Rennie Mackintosh handed over the Hill House to his clients, the Blackies, in a short ceremony in the spring of 1904. The family were to live in it, and love it, for the next half-century. Walter Blackie's *Memories*, published after his death by his daughter Agnes in 1968, has left us an illuminating and very personal account of the development of the house. It is the story of a relatively ordinary family living in an extraordinary house and the creative imagination of its architect.

The collaboration between Mackintosh and Walter Blackie (1860–1953) took place in the context of the rapid growth of Glasgow during the 19th century. This expansion generated a wealth and confidence that enabled entrepreneurs like Blackie to commission innovative work from protagonists of new, radical forms of architectural and decorative expression such as Mackintosh. For the architect, the commission was an unprecedented opportunity to design a large private villa from scratch, backed by an adequate budget and an open-minded client who gave him a great deal of freedom. Although both men made concessions, the rapport between them enabled Mackintosh to go beyond anything he had achieved in domestic architecture so far, and to realise an architectural masterpiece.

Blackie and his family could have had no doubt that Mackintosh would design something rather different from an ordinary suburban villa, and even from the more elaborate 'artistic' villas that were being built on the upper slopes of Helensburgh for other prosperous Glasgow businessmen. Blackie may also have been motivated by a desire to outshine his uncles, who had commissioned houses from Glasgow's great Victorian architect, Alexander 'Greek' Thomson.

Mackintosh's declaration at the handover ceremony implies that he had consciously moved away from reference to styles of the past and that he considered the best design to be based on functionality. Life and art, he believed, should be integrated. But the Hill House does not completely turn its back on architectural tradition. Sturdy old Scottish houses and castles are brilliantly evoked in the structure – sometimes literally, as in the spiral stair tower, and sometimes more abstractly, as in the way the intersecting gables at the south-east end play on the idea of turreted towers. And in the interior, the almost black panelling of the dining room suggests the dark, time-worn atmosphere of the great hall in a 17th-century castle.

Walter Blackie commented that Mackintosh had appeared to design the interior layout before turning to the external design. But, clearly, Mackintosh designed the exterior very carefully and calculated the precise effect the design of the inside would have on the external appearance of the building. He considered every detail as part of an overall aesthetic unity and developed a rich language of symbolic meaning and contrasting formal references, all of which form a dynamic and harmonious whole.

HOUSE AT HELENSBURGH
FOR W.W. BLACKIE ESQ.

CHARLES RENNIE MACKINTOSH (1868–1928)

Charles Rennie Mackintosh was born on 7 June 1868. He was the fourth child of Margaret Rennie and William Mackintosh, who had eleven children altogether, only seven of whom survived into adulthood. His father's gradual promotion in the City of Glasgow police secured the family's home life, leading to a rise in social status. Mackintosh appears to have developed a love for nature in early childhood – which was to be a source of inspiration throughout his life.

Apprenticed to the architect John Hutchison at the age of 16, Mackintosh took part-time classes at Glasgow School of Art to improve his drawing skills. His attendance there coincided with the appointment of the visionary Francis Newbery as director in 1885.

After five years' apprenticeship with Hutchison, Mackintosh joined the prestigious Glasgow architects Honeyman & Keppie in 1889 as a draughtsman. He won the Alexander Thomson Travelling Scholarship, which allowed him to travel on the continent, particularly in Italy, in 1891. His developing interest in the fine and decorative arts may have been encouraged by his introduction by Newbery to sisters Margaret and Frances Macdonald, who collaborated on metalwork, graphics and book illustrations. Together with Mackintosh's friend and colleague Herbert McNair, the quartet began to exhibit as 'The Four', gaining a certain notoriety with their unusual style. Reverting to symbolic meaning and organic shapes, this style had caused some less enthusiastic critics to dub the group 'the spook school'. An article in *The Studio* magazine in 1897 brought their work to the attention of architects and designers on the continent. Favourable foreign publicity and opportunities to exhibit abroad would, in the years to come, considerably increase Mackintosh's reputation on the continent and align him with the European artistic avant-garde.

A first commission for Miss Catherine Cranston's Buchanan Street Tea Room in 1896 marked the beginning of a patronage which would last over two decades. In the same year, and even more importantly, Honeyman & Keppie, with Mackintosh as designer, won the competition for a new Glasgow School of Art. The building was eventually completed in 1909 and would become a universally acknowledged masterpiece of early 20th-century architecture.

McNair married Frances Macdonald in 1899, and the following year Mackintosh married Margaret. The union led not only to private happiness but to professional success: commissions in Scotland and from abroad, exhibitions and collaborations with his wife, such as the international competition for the 'House for an Art Lover' in 1901, brought Mackintosh wide recognition and prestige. He was made a partner in Honeyman & Keppie in 1901, and in the same year he completed his first major domestic commission – Windyhill in Kilmacolm, Renfrewshire. This, together with his submission for the House for an Art Lover competition, paved the way for the design of the Hill House.

Commissions followed in Glasgow for the Willow Tea Rooms, the Ingram Street Tea Room and the Scotland Street School, and Mackintosh exhibited work in Turin, Moscow and Dresden. However, little work materialised after the completion of the School of Art in 1909: Mackintosh suffered from increasing ill health and seems to have become professionally unreliable. His partnership was dissolved in 1913 and the following year the Mackintoshes headed for Walberswick in Suffolk for an extended holiday with the Newberys.

Charles Rennie Mackintosh, 1893

Poster designed by The Four, c1895

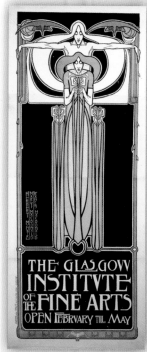

Above left: the library at Glasgow School of Art; top: drawing of House for an Art Lover; bottom: Willow Tea Rooms

But in 1915, a few months after the outbreak of the First World War, they were ordered to leave the area – Mackintosh's artistic connections with Germany and Austria had aroused suspicion in this uncosmopolitan locality. The couple settled in Chelsea, London, for a number of years, turning to textile design when architectural commissions – except for the design of a studio – were not forthcoming. Mackintosh supplemented a meagre income by designing book covers for his patron Walter Blackie.

For health and financial reasons, the couple decided in 1923 to move to the south of France. There, Mackintosh produced a series of around 40 superb watercolour landscapes intended for exhibition back in Britain. When his health deteriorated in 1927, Mackintosh travelled back to London, where he was diagnosed with cancer. Despite an operation and subsequent treatment he died there in December 1928, in comparative obscurity.

Mackintosh the architect, designer and artist was first rehabilitated in a memorial exhibition in Glasgow in 1933. Thomas Howarth's pioneering study in the 1940s, later published in his book *Charles Rennie Mackintosh and the Modern Movement* (1952), embodied new research and an important reassessment. The Mackintosh centenary in 1968 was celebrated with a major touring show at the Edinburgh International Festival, enhancing public awareness of his qualities as an interior designer. The founding of the Charles Rennie Mackintosh Society in Glasgow in 1973 and research – primarily that published in Roger Billcliffe's book, *Charles Rennie Mackintosh: the complete furniture, furniture drawings and interior designs* (1979) – heralded a rediscovery of the artist by his native city. As a cultural destination, Glasgow has now become almost synonymous with Charles Rennie Mackintosh, and today most of Mackintosh's buildings in Glasgow are well cared for and accessible to visitors. The Hill House, albeit outside the city, can claim to be the most complete and authentic jewel in the crown of his achievements.

Collioure, Pyrénées-Orientales – Summer Palace of the Queens of Aragon, a watercolour by Mackintosh, c1924–6

MARGARET MACDONALD MACKINTOSH (1864–1933)

'You must remember that in all my architectural efforts you have been half if not three quarters in them.'
(Letter from Charles Rennie Mackintosh to Margaret, 16 May 1927)

It may never be possible to assess the true extent of Margaret's influence on her husband's work, or every aspect of the couple's collaboration. Their shared life was most likely a very complex interaction in which boundaries were constantly shifting. However, comments like the one above suggest that Mackintosh had the highest respect for Margaret's creative abilities and seemingly acknowledges her influence on his work. After all, Margaret's art had come to some notice before she met Mackintosh at Glasgow School of Art around 1894, and she is now regarded as one of the most versatile, imaginative and successful artists working in Glasgow at the turn of the century.

Margaret Macdonald Mackintosh, c1900

These may also simply be the words of a man who loved his wife deeply and recognised the energy and the spirit he drew from this love. He also said *'Margaret has genius, I have only talent'*. She was a well of inspiration and a muse-like companion whose influence extended beyond her distinct contributions to the couple's collaborative projects.

The Hill House contains pieces by Margaret which stand as her work in their own right, as well as playing an important part in Mackintosh's whole concept. The decorative items she made for the house show her working in the two media in which she was most successful – gesso and embroidery. The gesso panel above the fireplace in the drawing room depicts the sleeping princess of the fairytale (detail opposite). The Blackie children's recollection of its making fuses Margaret's virtuoso technique with her unconventional appearance:

Above and below: details from copies of the intricate antimacassars designed by Margaret

'Mrs Mackintosh ... used a piping bag, like you would if you were icing a cake, and then stuck things onto the plaster. It was very beautiful. She seemed a big woman with a lot of red hair piled up under a hat with a pin through it. She wore what I'd call "artistic clothes" with baggy sleeves ... Mother liked her and they kept in touch.' (Agnes Blackie, 1989)

The antimacassars (now reconstructed) on the chairs and settle add splashes of colour to this predominantly white room, and bring a subtle vivacity and femininity to the interior. When Margaret came to make the curtains, she changed Mackintosh's design so that it would harmonise better with the rest of the room – clearly he agreed with her alterations.

Mrs Blackie admired Margaret's looks, her vivacity and independent manner and the two women got on well together. Family members recall enthusiastic discussions between Margaret and Mrs Blackie about the decoration of the house, reflecting the extent of Margaret's involvement with the project and the development of the relationship between the Mackintoshes and the Blackies.

Overall, Margaret's output was modest in scale and decreased as time went on. Her last known work, a watercolour of 1921, must have been painted when the couple lived in London, before they moved to France in 1923. Southern Europe was good for Margaret's health, and her small private income went further there, allowing them to live quietly and inexpensively. After Mackintosh's death in London in 1928, Margaret continued to travel between France and England. She died in her studio in Chelsea in 1933.

CHOOSING MACKINTOSH

'In the early spring of 1902 my wife and I, having decided to leave Dunblane where we had lived for some seven years, were fortunate enough to happen on the site at the crown of the hill in Upper Helensburgh where "The Hill House" now stands…. Fortune, again favourable, directed us to Charles Rennie Mackintosh for architect.'
(Walter Blackie, *Memories*, 1943)

Talwin Morris, art director at Blackie & Son, introduced Walter Blackie to Mackintosh in early 1902. Morris (1865–1911) was among the first to recognise and collect the work of 'The Four' – the group comprising Mackintosh, Herbert McNair, and Frances and Margaret Macdonald, and of which he was often viewed as the fifth member. He helped to popularise the particularly local variant of Art Nouveau that they adopted – the 'Glasgow Style', evident in his own cover designs on many of the books in the library at the Hill House.

Initially, Blackie feared that Mackintosh might be both too young and too distinguished – he had won plaudits for his design for the first phase of the new Glasgow School of Art – to take on his commission. In his early thirties, Mackintosh clearly still cut something of the youthful dash portrayed in Annan's well-known photograph of 1893, which shows a young man confident of his talent and making a certain self-conscious demonstration of his artistic inclinations. Yet Walter Blackie, by his own account, had watched the construction of the new art school with interest: it showed that Mackintosh was capable not only of tackling the technical challenges of a difficult site, but of combining a highly functional building with a totally new appearance.

Above: Glasgow School of Art; below: Willow Tea Rooms

Interestingly, in the late spring of 1902, Blackie's publishing house and Mackintosh both contributed to the International Exhibition of Modern Decorative Art in Turin, Italy. Blackie & Son were represented by selected book covers, including designs by Talwin Morris. Mackintosh was in charge of the overall design of the Scottish section and also produced the acclaimed 'Rose Boudoir' in collaboration with his wife. The artists for this important exhibition had been selected by Glasgow School of Art director Francis Newbery and showed Scotland at the forefront of modern design. The exhibition also included textile work by Mrs Blackie's younger sister, Jane Younger, who studied at the Glasgow School of Art.

After the first meeting between Walter Blackie and Mackintosh, an invitation quickly followed from Mackintosh to view a private villa he had completed in late 1901. Blackie wrote: *'An appointment at "Windyhill" was arranged and my wife and I were shown over the house by Mrs. Davidson, and left convinced that Mackintosh was the man for us.'* The Blackies thus joined a select band of clients, like the Davidsons and Miss Kate Cranston, who revelled in their patronage of a distinctive and highly original art style.

Windyhill was at that time the only villa in which Mackintosh had controlled both the internal and external design. This experience would feed directly into the Hill House – there remain strong similarities between the two houses – and, indeed become a starting point for much of its design. The Blackies' villa, however, also benefited from Mackintosh's participation in

Windyhill

the 'House for an Art Lover' competition. Although, or perhaps because, it was never built in his lifetime, this project allowed the architect's imagination full rein. In a bold move, and clearly inspired by their visit to Windyhill, the couple resolved to give Mackintosh full control over the design, decoration and much of the furnishing of four of the most important rooms in their new home. This was no meek gesture for an established household with perfectly acceptable furniture of their own!

But the architect had also been eager to assess his clients: *'Mackintosh came to see us at Dunblane, to judge what manner of folk he was to cater for'*, remembered Walter Blackie. The Blackies were a wealthy Glaswegian business family with, by the time they moved into their new house, five children. Walter Blackie sat on the board of directors of Blackie & Son and was in charge of the educational department, which published many children's books, including the popular fairytales. Blackie had joined the family business in 1884, became chairman of the company in 1919 and retired, after 53 years' service, in 1937. However, the company's prosperity diminished around the turn of the century, which perhaps explains some of the economies made by Blackie at the Hill House.

The earlier Blackies had already set a precedent for employing avant-garde architects: Alexander 'Greek' Thomson built the company's office in Stanhope Street, which included a studio designed by Talwin Morris. Walter's uncle Robert had been on the interviewing panel that appointed Francis Newbery as director of the Glasgow School of Art in 1885 – an appointment which was to be crucial to Mackintosh's progress. Robert Blackie was also one of the Trustees of the Alexander Thomson Travelling Scholarship, which Mackintosh won in 1890. Most importantly for the Hill House, Robert appointed Talwin Morris as art director to Blackie & Son in 1893, thus paving the way for the encounter between his nephew Walter and Mackintosh.

The peacock sconce, designed by Talwin Morris for the Hill House, with the entry in Mr Blackie's accounts showing how much he paid for it

DESIGNING THE HILL HOUSE

'I put to Mackintosh such ideas as I had for my prospective dwelling; mostly negative, I may say. I told him that I disliked red-tiled roofs in the West of Scotland with its frequent murky sky; did not want to have a construction of brick and plaster and wooden beams; that, on the whole, I rather fancied grey rough cast for the walls, and slate for the roof.'
(Walter Blackie, *Memories*, 1943)

Walter Blackie's 'wish list' stipulates building materials traditional to his country and expressive of its specific character. Here was a kindred spirit for Mackintosh, who himself was a fervent advocate of Scotland's architectural past. Such a gesture towards the principles of the Arts and Crafts movement – the use of local building materials and techniques – can be easily overlooked in the novel appearance of the finished product. In the interior of the Hill House, Mackintosh transformed this notion to a highly personal sense of place. There, many features are tightly interwoven with the immediate location of the garden, the hilly riverside and the occupants of the house.

The rootedness in the specific past and present of the location is an aspect of Mackintosh's work which sets him apart from most of the other architects working in Helensburgh (or even in Scotland) at the time. By comparison, nearby houses such as Brantwoode and Drumadoon, designed by one of the town's favourite architects, William Leiper, merely 'imported' English Arts and Crafts effects. They revel in the half-timbering, hanging tiles and red roofs of 'olde England', designed for clients intoxicated with southern tastes spread by publications such as *Country Life*. But neither did Mackintosh simply retreat to an idyllic adaptation of 'old Scots' revivalism, as did his contemporary Alexander N Paterson in his own home, The Longcroft, in 1901. Instead, he conjures up the 'feel' of a 'Scotch castle' without literally setting it out. He uses the hilly location to his advantage by emphasising the verticality of the building. The turreted stair tower, for example, and apparent L-plan of the highest portion viewed from the turreted gardener's hut unmistakably suggest an old tower house. This effect is further heightened by the all-encompassing harl, the hooded dormers, and the sparse and seemingly irregular arrangement of windows. These lend the exterior the robustness and austerity associated with old Scottish castles. Yet other elements, such as the advances and recesses of planes at the west façade, and the forceful angles of their chimneys, appear radical, almost proto-Cubist.

Drumadoon

The Hill House represents a union of two architectural opposites: traditional Scottish values and modern international aspirations. The architect's almost magical ability to distil new forms and shapes from traditional ingredients transforms the building into something completely innovative.

Blackie, who demanded from his architect that *'any architectural effect sought should be secured by the massing of the parts rather than by adventitious ornamentation'*, did little more than underscore his evident sympathy for what Mackintosh had already done at Windyhill. It clearly signalled to Mackintosh that his client was prepared to see this same theme developed on a grander scale. This was a promising start for an ambitious project.

MACKINTOSH AND THE VIENNA SECESSION

Articles in illustrated art periodicals such as *The Studio* brought the work of Mackintosh and his circle to the attention of artists of the Vienna Secession movement, leading to an invitation to show at the Eighth Secession exhibition in late 1900. The Secession was founded in 1897 by artists frustrated by the conservatism of the Austrian art establishment and its isolation from the rest of Europe. The group's aims and ideals were printed in the first issue of their magazine, *Ver Sacrum*. These included the running of an exhibition society which would promote the work of its members and Austrian art and attempt to break down barriers between fine and applied arts.

The Mackintoshes spent some time in Vienna, attending the opening of the exhibition in early November, and meeting various artists including Gustav Klimt, first President of the Secession. Herbert and Frances MacNair also submitted work. The group received particular acclaim for their whole room settings which included the pair of gesso panels designed by the Mackintoshes for Miss Kate Cranston's Ingram Street Tea Rooms. Reviews of the 'Scottish Room' were mixed, but as a consequence of taking part in the Eighth Secession exhibition, the group were invited to contribute to other international exhibitions such as Turin in 1902 and Moscow in 1903.

View of the 'Scottish Room' at the Eighth Secession exhibition

BUILDING A MASTERPIECE

Before long he submitted his first designs for our new house, the inside only. Not until we had decided on the inside arrangements did he submit drawings of the elevation. This first design was not approved. Thereupon, in a very few days he sent us a new set of drawings which were accepted, and soon the first sod was cut for the foundations of "The Hill House".'

(Walter Blackie, *Memories*, 1943)

NORTH ELEVATION

Blackie's memoirs suggest that Mackintosh may have taken more trouble than was usual to secure his client's agreement before finalising the plan for the exterior of the house. Although most architectural projects of the time took an integrated approach to the design of plan and elevations, Mackintosh seems to have gone that extra mile to put the internal layout, and with it the practical requirements of the family, at the heart of his design. However, it would be misleading to assume that Mackintosh did not, like other architects, have a keen idea of how the exterior would look as he went along. The harmonious design of the exterior undoubtedly reveals an eye for its aesthetic overall effect, albeit led by internal arrangements. After all, not long before, he had designed a smaller house of similar plan – Windyhill.

The design of the interior was concentrated on four spaces in particular. The economising patron did not want Mackintosh to design every single room in the house and decided that, rather than achieve the diluted effect of furniture 'sprinkled' all over the house, efforts would be concentrated on the drawing room, library, main bedroom and lower hall and staircase.

Despite this brief, every space in the house was given features such as skirting boards, fireplaces and stencilled decoration, which would link them sympathetically with the rest of the house. The upper hall, for instance, though devoid of individual pieces of furniture and plainly decorated, was consciously designed with a built-in seat recess – a private and restful space off the circulation area.

It appears that Blackie's rejection of the first design was due to both economic and aesthetic considerations: '… *I had brought it down to my figure by cutting out many details which could be done without, though in themselves desirable, as, for instance, the terrace, the retaining walls of the feu, the specially designed wrought-iron gates and many other details. But as the work progressed I got more and more in love with the discarded details and before we were done had restored practically all of them.*'

Opposite: the final phases of construction, 6 June 1903; left: Mackintosh's early drawings of the north and south elevations of the house; top: front and back views of the house in 1904; above: detail from the library

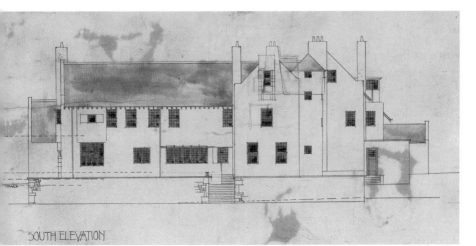

SOUTH ELEVATION

The features Blackie described now seem an integral part of the Hill House: their final readoption suggests that Mackintosh's design had an integrity which convinced even a rational mind of their necessity. But some features were categorically discarded, including the planned wrought-iron decoration hanging from the stone shutters of the windows in the main bedroom and the school room. These may have fallen into Walter Blackie's category of *'adventitious ornamentation'*, and the purging of such detail contributes to the sparse and plain external appearance of the building. Two interesting features abandoned in the interior were a proposed screen in the main bedroom, which was to separate the bed vault from the rest of the room, and a morning room between the drawing room and the dining room. The morning room was later incorporated into the drawing room as the music alcove. These changes – made in the dialogue between client and architect – made a vital contribution to the impact of two of the most important rooms in the house and gave them the spatial complexity they still have today.

Above: detail from a drawing showing Mackintosh's original idea for the ornamental ironwork for the bedroom window, which was rejected by Walter Blackie

Below right: Mackintosh's design for the main bedroom, showing the bed alcove with the embroidered panels on either side of the bed, and the washstand

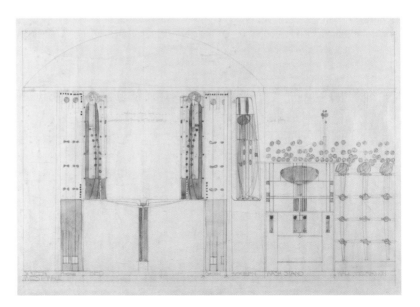

The arrival of the Blackies' fifth child in December 1903 demanded another adjustment – a linen cupboard on the first floor was sacrificed to make way for a larger bedroom accommodating two of the daughters. The most substantial alteration to the first design, however, was on the ground floor: a billiard room and a den to the north-west of the house, intended to give Walter Blackie an independent space to entertain male friends or business contacts, was never built for reasons of economy. Had this proceeded, it would not only have altered the use of the house, but would have considerably changed the external appearance.

The Blackies had specifically requested slate for the roof, and Mackintosh chose a blue-black variety from a Scottish quarry. Colour was not the only noteworthy feature of this slate. In contrast to the grey-green slate from England frequently used at other properties in the area, this Scottish variety was rougher and also less expensive. Often considered too coarse in texture for use on an imposing mansion, it was exactly what Mackintosh preferred.

In December 1903 the building was finally completed.

Mrs Anna Blackie and her daughter Agnes in the drawing room around 1910, before the ceiling was painted a darker colour

The Blackies' son, also called Walter, c1930

LIVING IN A WORK OF ART

'Mackintosh's rooms are refined to a degree which the lives of even the artistically educated are still a long way from matching. The delicacy and austerity of their artistic atmosphere would tolerate no admixture of the ordinariness which fills our lives. Even a book in an unsuitable binding would disturb the atmosphere simply by lying on the table …'
Hermann Muthesius (after a visit to the Mackintoshes' flat in Glasgow)

Friends visiting the Blackie children are reported to have believed their playmates were living in a monastery. This impression may have been created by the relatively plain wall decoration of the children's rooms, which were remembered as *'ordinary, albeit less cluttered'* than other people's. From the moment a guest entered the house, the hall and drawing room, with their careful ordering of objects, colour and space, must have appeared startlingly minimalist when compared to the more usual late Victorian or Edwardian 'artistic' interior.

But daily life at the Hill House, as remembered by family members, seems to have found a stable balance between the artistic and the practical. The children recalled a happy and carefree childhood and a distinct non-fussiness towards the use of the interiors. They remember that they were never told not to touch anything and that life in the house was quite normal. *'We never thought of it as something special. It was just our home,'* recalled Ruth Hedderwick and her sister Agnes Blackie in 1989.

As in any home, the Blackies put their stamp on the interior. *'Where there were white walls'*, the youngest daughter Agnes remembered many decades later, *'the family would add their own colour, largely by means of flowers.'* But it appears that the colour yellow was carefully avoided: *'Do you remember the fuss Mr Mackintosh made when mother put yellow flowers in the hall? He said ... it ruined his colour scheme.'* Pictures also helped. Ruth Hedderwick recalled that they were hung *'everywhere suitable'*, particularly in the east wing on the first floor and the schoolroom, the domain of the children.

When the family moved into the house in early 1904, Mrs Blackie and her sister Mary were on a convalescent tour of Switzerland and the Italian Lakes. Ruth, the oldest of the five children, was 14 and Agnes, the youngest, only three months. They brought with them household goods and furniture, some of which they sacrificed to allow Mackintosh to create distinct interiors. They did not, therefore, move into a fully furnished home: in fact, some of the new pieces were not yet even designed. Mackintosh supplied the furniture for the main bedroom in 1903, and throughout 1904 worked on moveable pieces for the hall and drawing room.

Once settled in, the family began to ask Mackintosh for additional pieces, such as the writing desk and the big cabinet for the drawing room, which were probably delivered as late as 1905. It was not until 1908 that Mackintosh designed a table for the drawing room – the famous cube table – and his wife Margaret made the intricate gesso panel above the fireplace. Mackintosh's last commission was to design a garden bench, in 1912: his involvement with the house had then spanned a whole decade, testifying to a consistent and lasting empathy between patron and architect.

The Blackies gradually became more acutely aware of the importance of the design of their home, as outside interest increased. Early on, recognition came only from a few specialist sources, mainly on the continent. But by the 1930s a change was apparent: Agnes Blackie remembered a visit to the house from the renowned architectural historian Nicolaus Pevsner. In the 1940s Thomas Howarth began his pioneering doctoral thesis on Charles Rennie Mackintosh which, for the first time, attempted a detailed study of Mackintosh's entire body of work. From the 1950s onwards, when the Lawson family moved into the house, interest gradually grew among academics, and eventually broadened into wider popularity from the 1990s onwards.

The four Blackie daughters – Jean, Ruth, Alison and Agnes, c1910

Designed by Mackintosh, the cube table was one of the last pieces commissioned for the house

There was not much trace in the Blackie family's daily life of the preciousness towards the interiors suggested by the German architect Hermann Muthesius. The children's free and easy childhood was similar to that of their Helensburgh neighbours: games in the house and garden, and picnics and excursions into the surrounding area. Bicycles, walking, the railway and steamers on the busy Clyde were the main means of transport. The Blackies had a superb view on to the river, particularly before the house directly to the south was built, and when many of the trees were in their infancy. Walter Blackie kept a telescope in the drawer of the right-hand window in the drawing room, to scan the view.

Like many of his wealthy neighbours, Walter Blackie 'commuted' to work in Glasgow. Ruth Hedderwick remembered processions of bowler-hatted men walking robot-like down Sinclair Street to Helensburgh railway station. 'Once I started running and the whole procession started running!', she recalled. Blackie was taken to the station in a horse-drawn cab, until he bought a car after the First World War. He would usually return from business by 7.30pm, at which time the main meal was served in the dining room. It was not a very formal affair. All the meals were taken here, including breakfast.

Apart from the cook, staff initially consisted of two housemaids, one table maid, a governess for one of the daughters, and a nanny. There was also a gardener, whose family were housed in the cottage on the premises. This small building, originally intended by Mackintosh to be more ambitious, was extended by local architect Robert Wemyss in 1928. Designed in a matching style, it may be the first example of mock-Mackintosh!

By the advent of the Second World War, social changes were affecting even Helensburgh's leafy, middle-class villa enclave – changes that were accelerated by the war itself. Evacuees from Clydebank were taken in to the house during the 1940s and accommodated in the children's wing.

With all their children, except Agnes, having married and left, the house was very big for the elderly couple and heating was expensive. Their daughters recalled later that it was probably Walter who was most reluctant to leave: 'Father liked Mr Mackintosh and he was devoted to the house. He never wanted to leave it.' Walter and Anna Blackie withdrew into the dining room for their everyday life. An armchair was placed at each side of the fireplace, the room was filled with furniture and books and was comfortably heated – here they had almost everything they needed. The drawing room was used only for special occasions. Walter lived here until his death in 1953, after which Mrs Blackie and Agnes moved out. The family had occupied the house for nearly 50 years.

Top: the gardener, Dow, with Agnes Blackie, c1908; middle: stencil detail in the drawing room; left: the Blackies kept hens and this photo, taken in August 1953, shows the hen runs in the garden

Clockwise from top left:
Mrs Anna Blackie, c1910;
Mrs Blackie and her daughter
Ruth in the library, April 1915;
before he bought a car, every
day a horse-drawn cab took
Mr Blackie to the station;
Agnes Blackie, aged around 4

AFTER THE BLACKIES

When the Blackie family left the Hill House in 1953, it was bought by
T Campbell Lawson, an accountant with a great interest in art. Along with
the house, the Lawson family bought some of the Mackintosh-designed
furniture. Although they made some alterations to the decoration and
changed the usage of certain rooms, the Lawsons took care not to undertake
any irreversible changes. When they put the house on the market again in
1972, they stipulated that it be sold with the furniture, which by then had
a value of £6,000. This appears to have deterred at least one buyer and
with no private sale forthcoming the Royal Incorporation of Architects in
Scotland (RIAS) agreed to buy the house in March 1972. The purchase price
was raised by an appeal, and a trust was formed to run it as a living house
rather than a museum.

When it became increasingly difficult to fund the upkeep of the building,
the trustees commissioned Glasgow architects Gillespie, Kidd & Coia to
subdivide the east part of the house into three self-contained flats for rent.
The Landmark Trust took over the top floor as a holiday let and in exchange
provided funding for five years. Further grant support was received from
various bodies, including the Historic Buildings Council for Scotland,
Dumbarton District Council, Strathclyde Regional Council and the William
Robertson Charitable Trust.

In 1982, after ten years under the RIAS, the National Trust for Scotland was
able to accept the offer of the house from the trustees. This was made possible
through the help of a generous endowment funded by the National Heritage
Memorial Fund.

The Hill House represented a very important addition to the property
portfolio of the National Trust for Scotland as one of its few 20th-century
buildings and its only building by Mackintosh. It joined an impressive range
of architecturally and historically significant buildings held by the Trust,
designed by architects such as Robert Adam, William Adam and
Robert Lorimer.

An exciting time of rediscovery began, and since 1982 the house has
been gradually restored to much of its original appearance. As the Trust,
in partnership with Historic Scotland, started to scratch the surface – quite
literally in those areas where paint scrapes were made – a surprising amount
of evidence was uncovered which sometimes challenged established views of
Mackintosh's design. The findings are by no means complete.

Most of the items of furniture on display in the main rooms are original pieces
that were designed for the Blackies. In those parts of the house for which
the Blackies commissioned no Mackintosh furniture, such as the east wing,
interpretation has been developed to explore the house in other ways. But the
Trust's chief aim – to restore those areas of the house where the Mackintoshes
decisively imprinted their character – has been achieved. There are now so
few authentic room settings elsewhere designed by the artist and his wife that
the Hill House is helping to fill an important gap.

TOUR OF THE HOUSE

'His purpose was not to be new, but to give fitting expression in design to a dwelling house of certain desired size, and meet the conditions of life of the occupants and he could not help being new and fresh however many hints or suggestions he may have received from great works of the past.'

(Walter Blackie, *Memories*, 1943)

23

LIBRARY

The library, just to the right of the entrance, was the ideal location for Mr Blackie to receive business callers without disturbing other family members. He worked here most evenings, catching the last rays of the setting sun. Purple glass insets in the door and the dark-stained oak furniture signal the masculine character of the room, while the stylised thistles above the fireplace, the slender reed curving up the front of the book cupboards and the carved motifs above the bookshelves all reflect his interest in nature and science. Pigeon holes above the fireplace held his pipe and tobacco, while the inbuilt cupboard and writing desk provided a convenient little office by the fire.

Oak bookcases line the walls to picture rail height. The volumes now on the shelves have been collected by the Trust and many were donated by the public. Those on the north wall were published by Blackie & Son Ltd and have their distinctive Glasgow Style bindings, some designed by Talwin Morris, who brought architect and patron together.

Walter Blackie, c1915

HALL

Panels of dark-stained pine around the stairway form a dark and mysterious place, an enchanted forest of fairy tales. Light from the stair window filtering through the tall staircase timbers catches the coloured glass insets which glow like jewelled wings. Four steps separate the lower hall from the main hall, protecting the family apartments from the casual caller. The hall is lit by large rectangular pendants decorated with representations of the honesty plant. Squares and rectangles are everywhere – in the dark oak furniture, in the intriguing organic motifs stencilled between the dark pine panels, in the carpet, the light fittings and in the glass insets in the doors.

The hall in 1904 and, opposite, the hall today

DRAWING ROOM

Moving from the dappled shade of the hallway, we enter the light and elegant rose garden that is the drawing room. Roses stencilled on the ivory white walls are separated by silver foil 'trunks', while stray petals are scattered as if blown in on a gentle breeze. On each side of the door frame Mackintosh provided a niche for slender vases of roses to scent the room – reinforcing the sense of an indoor garden.

The window seat in the south-facing bay window gave perfect light for reading as well as superb views of the Firth of Clyde.

The fireplace is made up of small putty-coloured tesserae decorated with petal-shaped mosaics in pinks and purples. In the corner, recessed shelves resemble the branches of a tree topped by pale purple and silver glass leaves. A creamy-white painted wooden mantel frames Margaret Macdonald Mackintosh's gesso panel, which depicts a sleeping princess in her protective bower of briar roses – another fairy tale reference, a recurring theme throughout the house. On the backs of two chairs and the fireside settle are copies of the intricate antimacassars, also originally designed and embroidered by Margaret.

To the left of the door, the music alcove has a low ceiling to provide a sounding board for the piano. Although not designed by Mackintosh, he did provide it with a new set of legs, in keeping with the other furniture in the room. The present piano replaces the original, which was lent in the 1940s to a convalescent home for wounded soldiers and not returned.

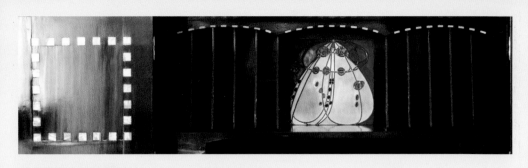

WRITING DESK

The most striking item of furniture in this room is the writing desk designed by Mackintosh for Mrs Anna Blackie. He liked this desk so much that he had a similar one made for himself. Mackintosh submitted three different drawings for the design of the writing desk in the drawing room. Walter Blackie settled on the last of these. After many years in a private collection, Mrs Blackie's desk was bought at auction in 2002 by the National Trust for Scotland in partnership with Glasgow City Council, with generous assistance from the National Art Collections Fund and the Heritage Lottery Fund. It now divides its time between the Hill House and Kelvingrove Museum in Glasgow.

DINING ROOM

In keeping with the taste of the time, almost all of Mackintosh's domestic dining rooms had dark walls with a lighter frieze and ceiling. He designed no furniture for this room as the Blackies wished to keep the furniture from their previous house in Dunblane. Of this, only two chairs and a side table survive along with the electric nickel-plated food warmer, which was donated by Miss Agnes Blackie. Mackintosh did, however, create the fireplace with its steel surround, and also the striking central light pendant, like a medieval stained glass jewel casket.

The portraits of Mr and Mrs Blackie, painted in the 1920s by Hilary Strain, indicate their very different personalities. Walter Blackie, relaxed, confident, pipe in hand, looks the viewer directly in the eye. Anna Blackie, shy and reserved, is absorbed in her book.

SERVICE QUARTERS

Beyond the door at the east end of the hall lie the kitchen and service quarters. Mr Blackie, in his notes about the house, praised Mackintosh's generous and practical provision of cupboards. In the butler's pantry, flower pantry and kitchen, he designed a range of cupboards for dishes and silver, paying as much attention to these as to less mundane parts of the house and ensuring that they were both functional and pleasing to the eye.

STAIRWAY

An alcove, so dim it is easy to miss, is tucked in to the left of the first flight of four steps on the main stairway. This seat was often occupied by the children as the perfect spying place to watch visitors to the house. Hidden behind the wooden uprights and swallowed up by the darkness, they could see without being seen. Above, on the half landing, light floods in through the tall windows with their stylised thistles reminiscent of heraldic badges. The magnificent light fitting is a perfect cube of metal and purple glass.

BATHROOM

On the first floor, between Mr Blackie's dressing room and the stairwell, is a state of the art Edwardian bathroom with luxurious bathtub and shower. Hot water pipes kept the room and the bath towels warm.

DRESSING ROOM

This small room, above the main door of the house, was Mr Blackie's dressing room. Mackintosh was asked to design a suite of furniture in mahogany to match a chest of drawers brought from Blackie's previous home in Dunblane – the spiral columns on the chest are copied on the bed.

The washstand with its decorative leaded glass splashback was recently returned to the house, generously gifted by Mr & Mrs Donald Taffner. The bed cover has been made from a panel embroidered in the Glasgow Style around 1905 by Jane Younger, Mrs Blackie's sister.

MAIN BEDROOM

Like the drawing room, the bedroom was designed with more than one function in mind. Mrs Blackie may have used it as a morning room, perhaps to sit reading a book on the fireside settle. Mackintosh had proposed delicate stained glass screens to hide the bed, but these were left out on grounds of cost. Instead, two black ladderback chairs subtly mark the change from one area of activity to another. The L-shape of the room also ensured privacy for the occupants of the bed under its barrel-vaulted alcove. Copies of Margaret Macdonald Mackintosh's silk embroidered hangings, made specially for Mrs Blackie and known to the children of the house as 'the skinny ladies', hang over the bed, which is lit by a tiny shuttered window in a curved recess.

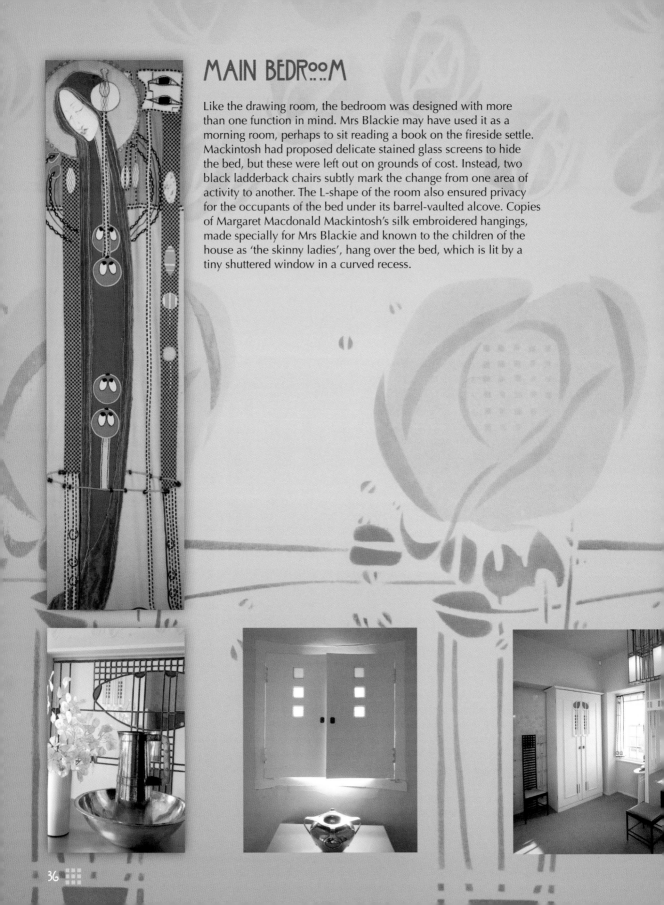

EAST WING

At the east end of the main corridor is the day nursery and the children's and guest bedrooms. Although Mackintosh did not design any furniture for these rooms, traces of the original decorative schemes have been uncovered which show his symbolism was as strong here as it was in the main rooms of the house.

Mackintosh also provided an alcove off the main corridor with fitted seats, which was used for sewing and also by the children of the house for playing dressing up. They kept their costumes under the seat lids.

Today, displays in the former bedrooms investigate Mackintosh's use of space, light, colour and texture. Two of the larger rooms are used for temporary exhibitions to show the work of new designers.

This Mackintosh-designed cupboard was acquired by the Trust in 2011. Made by Guthrie & Wells around 1896, it is believed to have been owned by the Blackies. As Walter recalled in 1943, 'Mackintosh came to see us at Dunblane ... I remember a strange happening just on his arrival. In the small entrance hall there stood an oak wardrobe or cupboard. Mackintosh ... told us that he had designed it. It was a strange chance that we should have been the purchasers; a good omen, it seemed.'

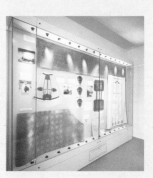

The drawing room, soon after the Trust took over the house in 1982, showing the dark painted ceiling

THE DRAWING ROOM UNCOVERED

The discovery of the original design scheme of the drawing room has been one of the most exciting chapters in the history of the Hill House. It shows the value of the work which the National Trust for Scotland, together with Historic Scotland, has achieved in this building. The 'white interior', long recognised as Mackintosh's signature, has been restored as a result of long and arduous research into its historical layers. It is hard to believe that until just over a decade ago the room had quite a different appearance, whose validity had not been questioned.

When the National Trust for Scotland took on the property in 1982 it was uneasy about the colour scheme in the drawing room that had been 'inherited' from the RIAS. It was also clear that a lot of the furniture then in the room had been borrowed because it was by Mackintosh, but had not been designed specifically for the Hill House. A programme of research was initiated to look afresh at the evidence which had guided the RIAS. New source material was identified, such as original drawings, Mackintosh's original workbooks, Blackie's household accounts and, very importantly, interviews with remaining Blackie family members and with descendants of workers who had been involved in the Hill House. A wealth of information emerged which eventually helped to establish a more complete understanding of the original room setting and decorative scheme.

When the RIAS took over the house in 1972, the walls of the drawing room were painted a brilliant white. The RIAS looked at contemporary black-and-white photographs, which revealed part of Mackintosh's original stencilled decoration. This was at first reconstructed without substantial evidence for its exact colouring. The result was a comparatively 'loud' decorative pattern, which in retrospect is easy to see did not sit well in the interior. The Trust, in turn, went back to the original prints, which revealed more detail. Closer examination of the underexposed photography from 1904 showed signs not only of fitted blinds in the window bay, but a completely different set of lights on the ceiling.

Left: the original ceiling light in the drawing room; above: one of the wall lights which replaced the ceiling pendant

The dangers of relying on a few surviving contemporary images had become clear. Fortunately, in the 1980s some members of the Blackie family were still alive and willing to be interviewed. The memories of two of the daughters, Agnes Blackie and Ruth Hedderwick, in particular, proved extremely interesting and useful, as did the recollections of Mrs Nancy Blackie, who had married the only son, Walter. The grandchildren helped as interviewers of their aunts, and also provided invaluable further information. These eyewitness accounts highlighted the very practical nature of many of the Blackie family's decisions about their living environment.

The lamps Mackintosh designed for the drawing room were one such example. Mrs Blackie, it turned out, had objections on practical grounds. She found that the lights radiated far too much heat for anyone sitting reading underneath them to be comfortable and, being gas, left dirt on the ceiling. Mackintosh was therefore asked to design something more appropriate. As early as 1905 the large cluster lights were taken down and replaced by the wall-mounted lamps that are still in place today. Sadly, the original lights have disappeared without trace.

The exact colour of the walls and the startlingly black ceiling also posed a real mystery. Early photographs of the drawing room clearly showed a white ceiling, but more material evidence was needed. The existing layers of paint and wallpaper were examined for traces of older decoration, and Mackintosh's workbook, held in the archives of the Hunterian Art Gallery at Glasgow University, was consulted. His notes revealed that in 1912 he had specified that the drawing room ceiling be repainted in a 'plum' colour.

Above and background: detail from Mackintosh's notebook of 1912, where he notes '... ceiling & frieze to be painted dark – shade to be a plum colour ...'

Again, the recollections of family members explained this drastic change. It emerged that Mrs Blackie had felt that the original cream-coloured ceiling was 'too infinite'. It may be that the replacement wall lamps revealed a much vaster uninterrupted expanse of bright ceiling than the original lamps; the white ceiling may also have proved impractical in a room with a coal fire and where Walter Blackie smoked his pipe. Mackintosh was called back to the house to repaint the ceiling.

Scrape tests showed that there were indeed still traces of white paint underneath the dark ceiling. On the walls, too, as the layers of paint and paper were gradually lifted, there appeared – albeit fragmented – a whole new world underneath. The pattern turned out to be differently placed and, importantly, to extend beyond what had been held to be the total scheme. The stencilled decoration on the west wall now extended into two column-like patterns reaching down to the floor. Interestingly, this could also indicate the original placing of furniture. The whole wall decoration was more detailed than had been previously thought. Stencilled traces of leaves, blades of grass and petals strewn across the walls began to surface, giving a much more subtly coloured decorative scheme. When one of the wall mounted lights was temporarily removed, it revealed yet another, apparently older, fragment of wall stencil.

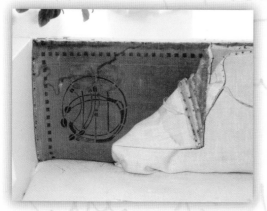

Uncovering the original stencilling on the window seat, February 1989

Analysis showed that the traces uncovered were of water-based paint, as opposed to the oil-based paint already uncovered in the rest of the room. The superimposed oil paint was eventually dated to the year 1912, when Mackintosh had returned to redo the ceiling. It may well have been asked for by the Blackies for practical reasons: oil-based paint could be much more easily cleaned.

The Blackies do not appear to have asked for further changes in this room after 1912. By 1953, when the Lawsons moved in, the paint on the drawing room ceiling had aged and appeared black rather than 'plum'. Quite legitimately, the new owners decided the ceiling simply needed a fresh coat of the same colour.

After extensive debate the Trust decided that the ceiling should be taken back to a cream colour as this had clearly been Mackintosh's original intention. It was felt that this was particularly important since so few of his original schemes survive. However, the Trust's conservation practice dictates that no restoration work should be irreversible, and that all legitimate traces of historic work should be conserved. So the original dark ceiling was not removed, but only covered. This will enable future generations to review their presentation of the house in the light of further research. Fragments of the original 1912 decorative scheme have been left exposed in this room to give an honest comparison of what is original and what has been replicated.

CONSERVATION IN ACTION: PROTECTING THE HILL HOUSE

As you look at the Hill House from the outside it is impossible not to notice cracks in the walls, and as you wander through the rooms you will see signs of damp. While this might look like neglect, it is a problem that seems to have affected the house since soon after its construction. In part this is because Mackintosh specified a relatively new product to protect the house from the harsh west coast weather – a harling made of Portland cement.

Such was his faith in this product that it may have influenced his decision to design the house with very few weathering details, such as projecting coping stones at roof level and overhanging window sills to deflect rainwater from the building. Unfortunately, nobody knew then that applying such a dense and brittle coating over the soft sandstone walls beneath was incompatible and would lead to cracking which let water in. Moisture is then trapped in the walls by the impervious cement coating, resulting in damp problems and damage to the precious interiors.

The Trust has done its best to manage the problem over the years by carrying out extensive roof and harling repairs, and internally by managing environment conditions and undertaking specialist conservation work to protect the fragile decorative schemes. Our expert buildings team are working to better understand the issues and how we can address this ongoing problem without compromising Mackintosh's unique design.

Thermal image of the dining room gable of the building; the green/blue areas indicate damp

THE GARDEN

While there is a wealth of information about the design of the house, we know far less about the original plans for the garden. Although Mackintosh normally viewed the grounds as an extension of the house, his involvement with the garden at the Hill House seems to have been minimal. Only a few features can be attributed to the architect; these include the 'lollipop' hollies, the unusual positioning of the rose garden next to the servants' quarters (to achieve a geometrical balance), and a series of gates and screens. We know that Walter Blackie was a keen and knowledgeable gardener and it is likely he had his own ideas about how the garden should look.

When the Trust acquired the house in 1982, the grounds were largely derelict. Weeds and self-seeded trees were rampant, the greenhouse was a ruin and the garden had become a wilderness. While the layout of the garden had changed little, not much of the original planting remained. Since then there has been an ongoing programme of renovation including, where possible, restoration of features of the early design and use of plants that would have been available in the early 20th century.

Opposite the front door is the half-circle lawn with its distinctive 'lollipop' hollies (*Ilex aquifolium* 'Scotica'), one of the original features suggested by Mackintosh. The central path is said to represent a tulip stem and flower.

Continuing down the western boundary are a series of garden 'rooms' including two 'plum pudding' rockeries (a characteristic of Edwardian gardens) and a small pond. Among the plants to be seen in this area are some outstanding Japanese maples, hostas, ferns and other shade-tolerant plants. In spring and summer, the pond attracts a variety of wildlife including frogs, toads, newts and dragonflies.

On the terrace to the south of the house are a number of specimen shrubs and small trees, with roses overhanging the terrace wall. Old photographs show shrubs trained against the wall of the house but these have not been reinstated because of the risk of damage to the façade.

Walter in his rose garden, c1915

The two lawns which dominate the south side of the garden are separated by a mature lime hedge. In 1982, the extensive lower lawn contained the remnants of a red blaize tennis court as well as a croquet lawn. Now, in spring a fine collection of daffodils flourishes in the lower lawn area.

The upper lawn is traversed by a curving path, to the right of which is a curious turfed mound of unknown origin. Miss Agnes Blackie remembered it being there when she was a child and it is possible that it covers a pile of stone and rubble left over from the building of the house. Once graced by a resplendent crab apple tree, now there are birch trees and, in spring, a succession of flowering bulbs including crocus, narcissus and bluebells.

A Mackintosh trellis arch leads from the herbaceous borders overlooking the eastern upper lawn to the wildflower orchard. Until the mid-1980s this was still maintained as an area of formal lawn. But old photographs show wildflowers growing here and these, together with a number of flowering crab and apple trees, were reintroduced. Some flowers such as fritillaries, cowslips, campions and hawkweeds have been deliberately planted while others, notably the spotted orchids, have found their own way in.

The lilac circle – a feature thought to have been suggested by Mackintosh – lies to the east of the house and contains the lilac *Syringa* 'Katherine Havemeyer' with an underplanting of blue-flowered periwinkle. Next to it is the rose garden. Laid out in the shape of a Celtic cross, the central beds once held a collection of hybrid perpetual roses surrounded by box hedging. But early in the 21st century the box succumbed to blight and the roses also started to deteriorate, so were replaced by a planting scheme of silver, blue and white perennials. Two of the peripheral borders in the rose garden contain a mixture of shrub and species roses underplanted with spring-flowering pulmonaria.

To the north of the house is a small kitchen garden and orchard. In the Blackies' day, all four plots in this area were devoted to the production of vegetables, fruit and cut flowers, but in 1984–5 the three largest plots were converted into an apple orchard. Many of the vegetables grown in the kitchen garden are varieties that were readily available in Victorian and Edwardian times. A small area behind the vegetable plot is reserved for growing cut flowers for the house.

At the rear of the house is a kinetic sculpture donated to the house in 1997 by the American George Rickey (right), who was a friend of the Blackie children in his youth. As well as this permanent sculpture there are, from time to time, other exhibitions of contemporary sculpture works in the garden.

WILDLIFE

In the birch woodland beside the car park the distinctive call of the willow warbler and the long-tailed tit can be regularly heard even if the birds show themselves only occasionally. Early morning visitors may even catch a glimpse of a roe deer grazing amongst the birch trees. The Trust carries out rhododendron clearance work here to conserve the woodland, and we hope this will develop into moss-rich oak woodland in time.

Below: the birch woodland behind the house; bottom: long-tailed tit

The Hill House itself has become home for breeding house martins who have made their nests above several windows. These nests do not damage the building and we are happy to have these international travellers set up home here.

The grounds are managed in a way that not only conserves wildlife but also integrates it into the garden design. Most notably, one of the main garden borders has dwarf cornel and bearberry, plant species now rarely seen in our hills but which complement the other garden plants and take advantage of the acid soils in the garden. The walls are also home to a pleasing variety of mosses and ferns, such as maidenhair spleenwort, hart's tongue and the delicate fronds of the lady fern.

As well as the wildflower meadow, the lawns have been allowed to retain a wild element, being home to species such as cuckooflower, heath bedstraw and field woodrush. The result of all this management is that the Hill House is home to many animals; it also attracts one of the Trust's favourite nocturnal visitors – bats. Survey work has shown that soprano pipistrelle bats regularly feed around the gardens and we are continually checking to see if they have established a roost in the house itself.

Geilston Garden

Main Road, Cardross, Dumbarton G82 5HD Tel: 0844 493 2219

A delightfully intimate and tranquil garden. Attractive features include the walled garden with its gigantic Wellingtonia tree, and walks along the Geilston Burn through the woodland. You can also buy fresh produce from the kitchen garden in season.

DIRECTIONS: On A814, 18 miles (29km) north-west of Glasgow
OPEN: 1 April to 31 October, 9.30–5, daily. Admission charge
DISTANCE: Approx 5 miles (8km) from The Hill House
FACILITIES: Picnic area; hot drinks; wheelchair access with assistance; car parking

Holmwood

61–63 Netherlee Road, Cathcart, Glasgow G44 3YU Tel: 0844 493 2204

This exquisite little gem was designed by Glasgow's other architectural genius – Alexander 'Greek' Thomson. Completed in 1858, the rooms are richly ornamented with themes from the classical world. Ongoing conservation work is gradually revealing more and more of Thomson's original decorative schemes.

DIRECTIONS: Off Clarkston Road, 4 miles (6.5km) south of Glasgow city centre
OPEN: 1 April to 31 October, 12–5, Thursday to Monday. Admission charge
DISTANCE: Approx 35 miles (56km) from The Hill House
FACILITIES: Shop; refreshments; picnic area; family activities; wheelchair accessible; car parking

The Tenement House

145 Buccleuch Street, Garnethill, Glasgow G3 6QN Tel: 0844 493 2197

Little has changed at this typical Glasgow tenement from the turn of the 20th century. Miss Agnes Toward lived here for over 50 years and you can see many of the original features, including the gas lighting, at this unique property.

DIRECTIONS: In Glasgow city centre
OPEN: 1 March to 31 October, 1–5, daily. Admission charge
DISTANCE: Approx 24 miles (38km) from the Hill House
FACILITIES: Shop; family activities; information available in multiple languages

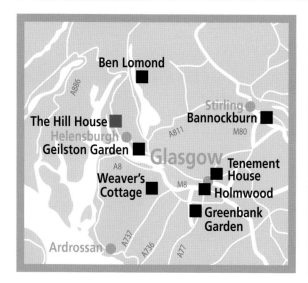

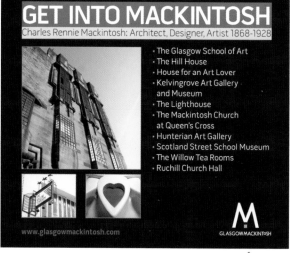